THE WORLD THAT WAS

By

C.D. Sharbono

THE WORLD THAT WAS

ISBN-13: 978-1492152804

ISBN-10: 1492152803

AtoZ Publishing Group, LLC

40 Plaza Way, 8-132, Mountain Home, AR 72653

Telephone: (870) 736-2548   Fax: (870) 492-7879

http://www.atozpublishinggroup.com

First AtoZ Publishing Group Printing August 2013

Published in the United States of America

ATTENTION: CORPORATIONS & ORGANIZATIONS

Most AtoZ Publishing Group books are available at special quantity discounts for bulk

purchases for promotions, premiums or fund-raising. For information, please call or write:

Special Markets Department, AtoZ Publishing Group, LLC

40 Plaza Way, 8-132, Mountain Home, AR 72653

Telephone: 870.736.2548   *   Fax: 870.492.7879

DEDICATION

This book is dedicated to my two sons, Jason and Justin Sharbono and their families as well as my foster boys, especially Jessie, who was fascinated with dinosaurs and prehistoric life and fossils.

Contents

INTRODUCTION

I would like to present a plausible explanation as to why planet earth and its prehistoric life forms are possibly millions of years old and yet present life forms, of which man is the last and highest of God's creation, are very young-probably 6,000-7000 years young. The concept of Lucifer and the fallen angels existing on planet earth, possibly millions of years before Adam and Eve were created, has not been expounded upon by scientific writers and only by a few religious writers. The Bible, more specifically Revelations 12:7-9, tells of a time when there was a war in Heaven. This war was between the godly angels, led by Michael, and the demon-like angels, led by Lucifer. This war ended with Lucifer and his band of angels being thrown out of Heaven. They possibly descended to planet earth during the Mesozoic era. It is interesting to note that scientific writers illustrate this era as being very beautiful and fruitful. This is reflected by so many fascinating and beautiful plants and magnificently huge creatures that are found fossilized in rock formations of the Mesozoic era.

Prehistoric earth (before any written record of historic events by humans such as Adam and Eve) was probably encircled by an ozone-like layer and possibly a water vapor layer. The effect of both of these layers and other atmospheric layers would have produced a green house effect. This in turn, would have supported the abundant prehistoric life that existed during the Mesozoic Era. Many scientists believe this era existed millions of years ago and lasted for millions of years.

The Hebrew Bible also indicates that the original planet earth was created beautiful. Isaiah 45:18 implies God's original creation was not created "tohou". Tohou, in Hebrew, means empty, void, desolate and/or without form. This verse in English then - means; "God did not create planet earth empty or void as well as God did not create planet earth formless. In fact, both Isaiah 45:18 and Jeremiah 4:23:27 indicate that the original planet earth was created beautiful and fruitful. Then in Isaiah 14:12-17, it indicates Lucifer was planning to ascend back into Heaven and take over God's throne. This was a rebellious scheme, (orchestrated by Lucifer), to usurp God's authority. This made God very angry. The Bible indicates that this rebellious scheme of Lucifer is the reason God destroyed prehistoric planet earth. These scriptures also indicate that God did not completely destroy or make a full end of planet earth at that time. However, this catastrophic destruction would probably have destroyed all life as we know it.

Many scientists believe a catastrophic event did take place at the end of the Mesozoic Era. They theorize that the mysterious disappearance of prehistoric life was caused by severe climate changes. One theory is that a giant meteor hit earth and exploded. Another theory is that there was an increase in volcanic and earthquake activity during this era. Either or both of these theories would have produced a world-wide dust cloud. As a result of either of these catastrophic events, the sun's light and thermal heat would have been clouded out or blocked. Note; without the sun's light rays and thermal heat - all life would die. Also planet earth would have been literally turned upside down as revealed by many land formations we presently see all around us

The Bible also indicates there was a lapse in time between God's original creation of planet earth and the partial destruction of earth's surface and the "re-creation" of the present atmosphere, landscape and life forms. Many religious scholars and writers refer to this lapse in time as "The Gap Theory of Creation". This lapse in time may have been thousands or millions of years. Scriptural evidence of this "Gap Theory" is found in Isaiah 45:18, Isaiah 14:12-17, Revelations 12:7-9, Jeremiah 4:23-27, Genesis 1:1-29 and 2nd Peter 3:5-7.

The Bible is the first written record of earth's history. God inspired the original writers of the Hebrew and Greek Bible books and gave them knowledge not only about revelation and prophecy but also prehistoric knowledge about planet earth. The "Gap Theory of Creation" is more clearly understood when we use the words found in the original manuscripts of the Hebrew and Greek Bible books. For example, in Hebrew, the word for "was" is "hayah" and it means; "became"; the Hebrew word "wilderness" is "tohou" and means;"empty, void, without form, desolate or in a state of confusion"; and the Hebrew word "moved" is "rachaph" and it means; "in deep thought". With these definitions in mind it is easier to understand the following scriptures. In Isaiah 45:18, Isaiah states "God made and formed the earth; He established it; He created it not void, not empty and not in vain; He formed it to be inhabited". In Isaiah 14:12-17, Isaiah states: How art thou (Lucifer) cut down to the ground, You who destroyed the World. For you (Lucifer) said to yourself; "I will ascend into heaven, I will exalt my throne above the stars of Heaven; I will be like the most High". (And) those who see you (Lucifer), will say; - is this the 'one' who made the earth to tremble; - who shook the kingdoms of this world; - who made the world as a wilderness (desolate, empty, void and in a state of confusion)? This concept is also stated in Jeremiah 4:23-27. In 2nd Peter 3:5-7, Peter states: The people deliberately forgot that - long ago by God's Word, the heavens that were of old and the earth that was of old, were standing out of the water and in the water; by these same waters the (old) world (that prehistoric world) was destroyed; and by this same Word, the present heavens and earth are kept in store, being reserved for destruction by fire on the day of judgment of ungodly people. Jeremiah states in Jeremiah 4:23-27; I beheld the earth, and lo, it was "tohou" (a wilderness, without form, empty, void and in a state of confusion). And the heavens, they had no light. I beheld, and lo, the mountains and hills, they trembled and shook. I beheld, and lo, the fruitful land (hayah) had become (tohou) a wilderness, desolate, empty and void (and in a state of confusion). The cities were crushed by the Lord-God's fierce anger. Then, this is what the Lord-God said; "The whole earth shall lay desolate; yet I, the Lord, will not make a full end or execute complete destruction (of planet earth).

Genesis 1:1 and 1:2 state; "In the beginning - God- created the heavens and the earth. And the earth (tohou) <u>became</u> void and without form - a wilderness - desolate and empty; and darkness was upon the face of the deep *(water)*. And the Spirit of God (<u>rachaph</u>) <u>moved</u> or was in deep thought.

In summary, prehistoric planet earth was first made beautiful and fruitful. Lucifer appeared on planet earth sometime in the <u>very distant past, (way) before Adam and Eve were created</u>, possibly during the Mesozoic Era when dinosaurs were abundant. Then Lucifer rebelled against God. This rebellion of Lucifer made God fiercely angry - so God partially destroyed prehistoric earth, His original creation. But, God did <u>not</u> execute complete destruction of earth. Planet Earth may have physically existed in a desolate, empty, void condition for millions of years while God (<u>rachaph</u>) <u>moved</u>, or was in deep thought, or hovered over the deep (water). God may have been "<u>moved</u>" to create a human being (in His likeness) who could and/or would communicate with Him - willingly. Also, during this period of time - the Lord God could have been in deep thought as to how He could or would save His soon to be newly created ones (humans) if they disobeyed or rebelled or sinned against Him. This would have been the time between Genesis 1:1 and Genesis 1:2 or, before God began to <u>recreate life</u> as we know it today; Genesis 1:3-29. This lapse in recorded time would have provided ample time for the carbon and hydrogen ions of animal fat (most likely dinosaur fat) to chemically change into the carbon - hydrogen molecules of the oil and gas supplies that we find so abundantly in planet earth's crust - today. Would it not be interesting to be able to calculate how many dinosaurs were immediately buried (without oxygen) in order to form the oil and gas we now use day, by the barrels, for energy!!

C.D. SHARBONO

THE WORLD THAT WAS BEFORE ADAM & EVE!

There was a different planet earth - millions or maybe even billions of years ago. It was different than this present earth age. There were different looking birds, insects, amphibians, fish, reptiles, mammals, plants and possibly even giants with wings (cherubs).

Scientists have divided past earth ages into three ages. These earth ages are: the Paleozoic Age, the Mesozoic Age and Cenozoic Age. The Mesozoic Age is further divided into three periods which are: the Triassic, Jurassic and Cretaceous periods.

It was probably during the Mesozoic Age that Lucifer and the cherubs lived on planet earth and ruled it. They may have built cities. The Jurassic period, which is in the middle of the Mesozoic Age, is known as the period or age - of - dinosaurs. This is because large numbers of various species of dinosaurs lived on planet earth during this period. From fossil evidence, this period was warm and tropical. Fossil evidence also implies that period must have had a healthy supply of oxygen for the animals to use and carbon dioxide for the plants to thrive; in other words that prehistoric age supported an abundant number of species, both plants and animals- though different from what we see on planet earth today.

Jessie had often dreamed of living during the age of dinosaurs. He read extensively about prehistoric life on pristine (unspoiled by pollution) planet earth. He felt it would be great to possibly tame the dinosaurs and ride on their backs as they roamed over pristine - planet earth. So, one night Jessie went to bed with a really big wish and that was to visit

planet earth during the Mesozoic Era.

Jessie woke up during his dream and found himself surrounded by herds of dinosaurs. It was beautiful and fantastic. All of a sudden Bronto, the Brontosauraus, and a large herd of dinosaurs came very close to him. He knew their names. Stego, the Stegosauraus; Allo, the Allosaursus; Coelurus, the Coelurus; Tyrano and Rex, the Tyrannosaurus brothers; Ptero, the Pterodactyl; Trico, the Triceratops and Anko, the Anklosaurus; Maia, the Maiasaurus; Salta, the Saltasaurus; Cory, the Corythosaurus; Archo the Archaeopteryx; Campo, the Camptosaurus. They all were keyed up, and talking amongst themselves. They were all concerned about what the Most-High was going to do to Lucifer and his band of winged beings since Lucifer was becoming more rebellious and arrogant.

Stego: "I'm getting very concerned about Lucifer's attitude. He is getting mighty 'cocky' and disrespectful of the Most-High"

Coelur: "I believe you are right Stego. I over-heard Lucifer talking to some of those other beings-with-wings. Lucifer told them; "I ascend into heaven and I exalt my throne above the stars of the Most-High."

will
will

Ptero: (interrupts)

 "Who is Lucifer?"

Rex: "Lucifer was the Most-High's favorite creation. Of course that was before Lucifer and one third of the beings-with-wings were thrown out of Heaven. You all know that there was a war in Heaven, and Lucifer lost! That is when the Most-High expelled Lucifer and his band of winged beings. It was basically because of Lucifer's rebellious nature. He wanted to usurp the Most High's authority and rule Heaven and Earth." This band eventually landed on planet earth thousands of years ago - by my recollection.

Ptero: "Now I know!!! Lucifer is  the leader of those beings-with-wings. Lucifer is the very handsome one, but he is not very wise. In fact, Lucifer and his band are the one that are responsible for building those cities and damming up many of our natural water ways. They have destroyed much of our natural habitat that we have enjoyed for thousands - actually maybe even millions of years."

Tyrano: "You know, we should come up with a more reliable method of dating those rocks. The Most-High could create beings - who, in the future, might get it right. But, right now, those beings-with-wings use the 'uranium to lead' method of dating rocks.

Of course, that method of dating rocks makes our planet earth millions or billions of years old. But when they use the 'krypton to argon' method of dating the very same rocks, they get our planet to appear much younger. The 'uranium to lead' method of dating earth rocks is based on the assumed fact; that in the very, very beginning of planet earth, all the rocks contained only uranium and <u>no</u> lead." HOW IGNORANT OR INSANE IS THIS!!

Their conversation then drifted back to Lucifer and the other beings with wings.

Allo: The ones that dwell in the nearby cities seem to be in charge of an energy system all their own. This energy system is very unique - because some periods of light seem to last a very long time and  during other periods - the period of light is very short.

Coelur: Well, this may be because the Most-High has not yet made a Sun to rule the day  or a moon to rule the night. It is almost like we live in a warm tropical bubble here on planet earth.

Maia: "I heard Lucifer say; "I will be like the Most-High, and I will sit on the mountain of the assembly in the sides of the north".

Trico: "Why the north?"

Bronto: (slowly and wisely) "The north is where the Most-High sits. The north represents His throne and that is why we should do something about this situation on planet earth; before the Most-High gets angry enough to really make some drastic changes on planet earth. These changes might hurt us and might even cause our extinction.

Stego: "What do you think the Most-High will do? What kind of changes can he possibly make? We all know there hasn't been any changes on earth since we were created.

There is still just one land mass. And those strange beings call it Pan-gae-a. It has been surrounded by this large body of water called the Panthalassa Ocean. We have seen those pointed like mountains spew out foul, smelling smoke and ashes for years.

Trico Jr.: "We've seen the same inland sea's called lakes or ponds. Also, for years we have seen the same plants, birds and all the other animals with whom we have shared our resources".

Maia: "Well! I don't believe the Most-High even knows or cares about what is going on down here on planet earth."

Trico: "Why?"

Anklo: "Because, if He really cared, He would have done something with Lucifer by now."

Campo Jr.: "I fear that the Most-High is just going to get tired of all of Lucifer's activities or shenanigans and really do something drastic. We might even get hurt or even die!

Coelur: "Now just how could anyone cause something that drastic? The Most-High would literally have to turn this planet upside down or inside out. And you know that would take a mighty big force."

Allo: "All those steaming mountains could keep on spewing out that foul smelling gas, smoke and hot liquid. If that continued it would darken planet earth and we would not be able to see anything. That lava could also push all the plants into nearby valleys and cover them up. This would not only cover up our inland seas and fresh water resources, but would destroy our supply of food and oxygen. It could also bury us and with all this fat, that we are made of, would become gas and oil. Just think about that fact because then we would become an important energy source for Lucifer and his band."

Dimo: "If this happened, planet earth as we know it would perish. Also, I believe the Most-High might let all those plants set covered up for millions of years. These plants would then turn into coal. Then those beings with wings would have another large source of energy in that new and probably different earth age."

Campo: "If that hot liquid (you all call lava) would fill up all the valleys and inland seas, then the ocean water would rise and flood this entire earth."

Pachy: "We can't live here if all those mountains explode and continue to spew out that terrible foul smelling gas, ashes and hot liquid."

Salta Sr.: "I'm just not going to be concerned about any of this stuff. I will just choose to believe - life will go on as it has for millions and/or billions of years."

Allo: "No! No. We all need to get together and go to the city to talk to Lucifer; to plead with him to be more satisfied and content with ruling his kingdom here on planet earth. I think that planet earth is beautiful and perfect just the way it is. In fact, we truly live in a warm, tropical greenhouse bubble. The temperature and conditions are tropical year after year. That is the reason we have all these lushes green tropical plants to eat."

Bronto: "Yes we need to talk with Lucifer, because I know we can't live here long if it freezes. I like it just the way it is right now. However, I do believe it was very cold in the past and that there was an ice age before we were created. That is because I can see the evidence of glacier activity all around. That era must have been really cold. And I don't even want to think about what would happen to me if it were to freeze again."

Archo: "Lucifer is the Most-High's favorite creation and He's not going to let anything bad happen to Lucifer or those other beings-with-wings. Look how beautiful they all are - especially Lucifer.

Campo #2: "I think one of those meteors from outer space could come crashing down and knock planet earth into  a different orbit. If this occurred, the temperature would certainly get so cold that snow and ice would collect to form glaciers again. Either way, though, we would not survive and all of us would become extinct."

Tyrano: "Well I know one thing for sure: if the Most-High does something and all these life forms including us become extinct, He could start over and make a new  earth age with new kinds of living things, both plants and animals. In fact, His new creation may be smarter than we are."

All of a sudden, Jessie heard a very loud explosion in the distance and then the mountains began to shake and spew out huge amounts of ash and hot liquid. It pushed all the vegetation and prehistoric animals, even the huge dinosaurs, into the existing valleys and inland lakes. It covered them immediately with large quantities of lava and earth.

Jessie then began to surmise that the huge numbers of fatty dinosaurs, pushed into the inland seas and valleys and covered immediately without a source of oxygen to decompose their bodies into water vapor and carbon dioxide, would begin forming the large oil and gas deposits from the carbon and hydrogen ions of their fat. Also, Jessie began to calculate how many dinosaurs it

 would take to fill up their car's gas tank....

Now, we find the Most-High is hovering over the deep (water) and brooding - in great thought.

Wow! Look what the Most-High has on his mind?

REFERENCES: King James Bible

2nd Peter 3:5-7 Where-by the World that then was, being overflowed with water - perished. But the heavens and the earth, which are now, by the same Word of God are kept in store, reserved unto fire against the day of judgment.

Isaiah 14:12-17 How are thou fallen from heaven, O Lucifer, son of the morning; For thou has said in thine heart, I will ascend into heaven, I will exalt my throne above the stars of God; I will sit also upon the mount of the congregation, in the sides of the north; I will ascend above the heights of the clouds; I will be like the most high.

You shall be brought down to Sheol, to the lowest depths of the pit. Those who see you will gaze at you, and consider you, saying; Is this the man who made the earth tremble, who shook kingdoms; Who made the World (tohou) as a wilderness and destroyed its cities, who did not open the house of his prisoners?

Jeremiah 4:23-27 I beheld the earth, and indeed it (hayah) was made to become without form and void; and the heavens, they had no light. I beheld the mountains, and indeed they trembled, and all the hills moved back and forth. I beheld and indeed there was no man, and all the birds of the heavens had fled. I beheld, and indeed the fruitful land (hayah) became (tohou) void, a wilderness, desolate and empty. For thus says the Lord; "The whole land shall be desolate; yet I will not make a full end."

Genesis 1:2 And the earth (hayah) became (tohou) without form and void; and darkness was upon the face of the deep. And the spirit of God moved (brooded) upon the face of the waters.

Isaiah 45:18 For thus saith the Lord - that created the heavens and formed the earth.   He hath established it. He created it not (tohou) desolate, empty, void or in vain.

Hebrew Definitions:
   Hayah; was sometimes interpreted to be "was" but meant "became or to become".
   Tohou; can mean any of the following; void, without form, empty, vain, or wilderness.
   Rachaph; was interpreted "moved" but meant "brooded or in deep thought".

Note: Lucifer is another name for Satan or evil one or morning star. He took 1/3 of the angels out of heaven thousands or millions of years before Adam and Eve were created. He descended to earth sometime in the dateless past, (prehistoric). He then tried to ascend back into heaven - above the clouds - and take over God's throne. It was this rebellion against God's authority that made God angry enough to destroy His original creation on planet earth - that is referenced in 2nd Peter 3:5-7

DINOSAURS

Camptosaurus, 20 ft (6 m) long, from Europe and North America

Allosaurus, 39 ft (12 m) long, from North America

Stegosaurus, 30 ft (9 m) long, from North America

Coelurus, 7 ft (2 m) long, from North America

Saltasaurus

Tyrannosaurus

Triceratops

Corythosaurus

Pachycephalosaurus

Euoplocephalus

DINOSAUR FACTS

#1: What is a Dinosaur? When scientists talk of dinosaurs, they <u>**mean a unique kind of creature that lived on land during the Triassic, Jurassic, or Cretaceous period.**</u>

#2: What are the Ages of Dinosaurs? They are Triassic, Jurassic and Cretaceous.

#3: The Smartest Dinosaur was The Troodon! Scientists measure smartness by figuring out how big an animal compared to its body. This is called "encephalization quotient." Troodon wins! Even so, they think he was only about as smart as a modern possum.

#4: The Dumbest Dinosaur was The stegosaurus! It had a brain as big as a walnut in a body weighing nearly two tons! A nicer way to say this is: Stegosaurus was "less smart" than a Troodon!

#5: The Fastest Dinosaur was Coelophysis and other Ornithomimosaurs. Scientists think these dinosaurs ran up to 30 miles per hour for short distances!

#6: The Biggest Dinosaurs were Saurpods: Seismosaurus was 165 feet long with tail. Arentinosaurus was the heaviest at 100 tons. The Brachiosaurus was 39 feet high (which helped it reach branches in trees). Giganotosaurus was the largest hunting dinosaur, at 46 feet long and up to 8 tons!

#7: The Smallest Dinosaur was the Saltopus. It was only 3 feet long, and weighed about five pounds.

#8: What Killed the Dinosaurs? No one really knows! Scientists have several theories:

> Meteor hits the earth!
> Lots of volcanic eruptions!
> Climate Changes (over a long period of time)

#9: Dinosaurs Lived on Land! Many prehistoric sea creatures lived at the same time as dinosaurs. However, they were not true dinosaurs! <u>Kronosaurus was believed to be the largest of all the sea reptiles.</u> It grew to be almost 42 feet long.

#10: Dinosaurs First Appeared in the Triassic period, around 200 million years ago. A group of reptiles from the late Permian Period (archosaurs) became the best hunters on land. They developed special features in their skulls and how they walked (having an upright body with their legs under their body), which made them dinosaurs.

#11: What do Dinosaur eggs look like? Dinosaur eggs have many shapes and sizes. Some eggs have been documented to be 16" long or more. The first dinosaur egg fossils were found in France in 1869. Many dinosaur eggs found still have their original shells.

DINOSAURS TO COLOR

FOSSIL FUEL (Crude Oil, Natural Gas and Coal)

Fossil fuels (crude oil and natural gas), were once alive! They were formed from prehistoric plants and animals that lived probably millions of years ago; way - way - before man, as we know man, was created.

Think about what the Earth must have looked like millions of years or so ago. The land mass we live on today was just being formed. Probably there were swamps and bogs everywhere. The climate was probably warmer and ancient trees and plants grew everywhere. Fossils indicate strange looking animals walked on the land, and just as weird looking animals swam in the rivers and seas. Tiny one-celled organisms called phyto-plankton floated in the ocean and fern-like plants grew both in the water and on the earth's surface.

When these ancient living things died, especially in huge numbers; they became buried in an "anaerobic environment" (i.e., an environment without the presence of oxygen) under layers and layers of mud, rock, and sand. Eventually, and maybe suddenly, hundreds and sometimes thousands of feet of earth covered these once living, fat containing - creatures that represented prehistoric life. (Prehistoric life refers to life that existed on planet earth before the written word was developed and/or before man as we know man -existed; that is humans who have 46 chromosomes and a genetic code like what we have today. This genetic code, for example, has genes for eye color located on the same chromosome and at the same gene loci (address). If there was another animal with 46 chromosome but their genes for eye color were on different chromosomes and at different gene loci then that creature would not be human).

During the millions of years (eras) that may have come and gone, these dead plants and animals slowly decomposed and formed the fossil fuels that we use today. Different types of fossil fuels are formed depending on the combination of animal and/or plant debris that was buried, how long that material was buried, and what conditions of temperature and pressure existed when they were decomposing in that anaerobic environment.

For example, oil and natural gas were created from organisms that lived and/or died in a water environment and were buried under layers of ocean or land sediments. Long after the great prehistoric seas and rivers vanished or dried-up, heat, pressure and bacteria combined to compress and the organic material under layers of silt. In most areas, a thick liquid called crude oil formed first, but in deeper, hot regions underground, the heating process continued until natural gas was formed. Over time, some of this oil and natural gas began working its way upward through the earth's crust until they ran into rock formations called "cap-rocks" that are dense enough to prevent these liquid fossil fuels from seeping to the surface. It is from under these "cap-rocks" that most oil and natural gas is extracted today.

Similar types of forces created coal, however the biggest difference is - Coal formed from the dead remains of <u>vegetation</u> (i.e., trees, ferns and other plants) that thrived during the pre-historic eras. In some areas, such as portions of what-is-now the eastern United States, coal was formed from swamps vegetation and was covered by sea water. Sea water, back then, must have contained a large amount of sulfur; and as silt eventually covered the various types of prehistoric vegetation and the seas dried up, the sulfur was left behind in the coal, usually under silt or sand-stone rock. Today, as part of the coal mining process, scientists are busy working on ways to take the sulfur out of coal. This is because when coal containing sulfur - burns, the sulfur can become an air pollutant - forming sulfuric acid. Some coal deposits, however, were formed from freshwater swamps which had very little sulfur in them. These coal deposits are located largely in the western part of the United States and this coal does not have sulfur in them or if it does, it is very little.

Note: It takes 200 feet of plant (vegetative) material (i.e., leaves and wood) to make 40 feet of coal.

Oil

Oil is basically any neutral, non-polar carbon-hydrogen containing chemical substance, that is a viscous (thick) liquid at present biotic temperatures. It is immiscible with water but soluble in alcohols or ethers. Oils have a high carbon and hydrogen content and are usually slippery to touch and very flammable. Oils may be animal or vegetable in origin, and may be volatile or non-volatile. Note; volatile refers to the fact these chemicals can evaporating rapidly in the form of vapor and non-volatile means that these organic chemicals do not evaporate or vaporize readily.

Types: (Mineral oils and Organic oils)

Mineral oils refer to crude oil, or petroleum, and its refined components are collectively known as petrochemicals. Petrochemicals or crude oils are crucial resources in our modern economy. Crude oil originates from ancient fossilized organic materials, such as zooplankton, algae, whales, fish as well as land animals such as dinosaurs and other "fat" containing animals or plants that died in large numbers and were buried immediately in an anaerobic environment (an environment that contains no oxygen) usually in ancient seas. Then, due to geochemical processes (heat and pressure) over many years, these organic sources were converted or changed chemically into oil. The name, mineral oil, is a misnomer in that minerals are not the source of mineral oil;- ancient plants and animals are the source of mineral oils/crude oils! Minerals are technically not organic. Mineral oil is organic. However, it is classified as "mineral oil" instead of as "organic oil" because its organic origin was very remote at the time of its discovery. Note; Mineral oils/Organic oils are obtained in the vicinity of rocks, underground traps, and sands.

Organic oils are technically not mineral oils. Organic oils are more correctly known as cooking oils. These oils are more associated with present or living animal or plant life. They are usually "edible" products. Also, they are produced by remarkably diverse groups of plants, animals, and other organisms through natural metabolic processes. Lipid is a type of organic oil that is not directly used for cooking. It is the scientific term for fatty acids, steroids and similar chemicals often found in the oils produced by living things. Organic oils may also contain chemicals other than lipids, including proteins, waxes and alkaloids.

Both mineral oils/crude oils and edible organic oils have a high carbon and hydrogen content and do not contain oxygen or are considerably lacking in oxygen compared to other organic compounds.

Applications of oils

Cosmetics: Oils are applied to hair to give it a lustrous look, to prevent tangles and roughness and to stabilize the hair to promote growth.

Religion: Oils are commonly used in ritual anointments. As a particular example, holy anointing oil has been an important ritual liquid for Judaism and Christianity.

Painting: Color pigments are easily suspended in oil, making it suitable as a supporting medium for paints. The oldest known existing oil paintings date from 650 AD.

Heat transfer: Oils are used as coolants in oil cooling, for instance in electric transformers. Oils are also used to enhance heating in other applications, such as cooking (especially in frying).

Lubrication: Oils are commonly used as lubricants. Mineral oils are more commonly used as machine lubricants than biological oils are. Whale oil is preferred for lubricating clocks, because it does not evaporate, leaving dust, although its use was banned in 1980. As no suitable substitute is available, whale oil is still used in space (in small quantities).

Note: In the 18th and 19th centuries, whale oil was commonly used for lamps, which was replaced with natural gas and then electricity.

Fuel Oil: Some oils burn in liquid or aerosol form, generating light, and heat which can be used directly or converted into other forms of energy such as electricity or mechanical work. To obtain many fuel oils, crude oil is pumped from the ground and is shipped via oil tankers to oil refineries. There, the crude oil is converted into diesel fuel (petro-diesel), alkanes (ethane, propane, etc.), fuel oils (the heaviest of commercial fuels are typically used in ocean liners/furnaces), kerosene, benzene , gasoline (petro),as well as jet fuel and liquefied petroleum gas. Note: Alkanes consist only of hydrogen and carbon atoms in which all bonds are single bonds and the carbon atoms are not joined in cyclic structures but instead form an open chain.

Note; A 42 gallon barrel (U.S.) of crude oil produces approximately 10 gallons of diesel, 4 gallons of jet fuel, 19 gallons of gasoline, 7 gallons of other products, 3 gallons split between heavy fuel oil and liquefied petroleum gases, and 2 gallons of heating oil. Not all oils used as fuels are mineral oils/crude oils. One example is corn which is now being used to make <u>biodiesel</u> and <u>vegetable oil fuel</u>.

Crude Oil and its chemical structure

The smallest unit of a substance, which still retains the characteristics of that substance, is called a molecule. Molecules can only be divided into atoms. - Atoms are different elements. For example, all molecules of water are identical and have the characteristics of water. The two atoms of hydrogen and an atom of oxygen (which make up a molecule of water) on their own have none of the characteristics of water.

Crude oils are <u>mixtures</u> of many different molecules and they are often difficult to separate. However, crude oils can be separated during the refining process to yield the various petroleum products such as: gasoline, kerosene propane, fuel oil, lubricating oil, wax, and asphalt. These substances mainly consist of compounds that have only two elements: carbon (C) and hydrogen (H). Therefore, they are called "hydrocarbons".

Refining crude oil involves two kinds of processes to produce the products that are so essential for energy in our modern society. First, there are physical processes which simply refine (separate) the crude oil (without altering its molecular structure) into useful products such as lubricating oil or fuel oil. Second, there are chemical or other processes which alter the molecular structure and produce a wide range of products such as cosmetics, oil base paints, etc., and most of them are known by the general term petrochemicals.

Crude oil can be refined into a wide variety of hydro-carbons/petrochemicals. Petrochemicals are the refined components of crude oil and the chemical products made from them. Petrochemicals are used as detergents, fertilizers, medicines, cosmetics, paints, plastics, synthetic fibers, and synthetic rubber.

Hydrocarbons are petrochemicals and petrochemicals are hydrocarbons. Hydrocarbons may be gaseous, liquid, or solid at normal temperature and pressure, depending on the number and arrangement of the carbon atoms in their molecules. Those molecules with up to 4 carbon atoms are gaseous; those with 20 or more are solid; those in between are liquid. Crude oils are liquid but may contain gaseous or solid compounds (or both) in solution. Heavy crude oil is usually a liquid at room temperature, however, as the temperature cools and the number of carbon atoms each molecule contains increases, the closer it is to being a semi-solid or solid (i.e. the more carbon atoms its molecules contain makes it more likely to become a solid at cool temperatures). Light oils (those that contain only a few carbon atoms) will remain liquid even at very low temperatures.

The simplest hydrocarbon is methane, a gas consisting of one carbon atom and four hydrogen atoms. Propane is a straight chain molecule with 3 carbon and 8 hydrogen atoms. Iso-butane is a branched chain molecule consisting of 4 carbon and 10 hydrogen atoms. More complex molecules occur when one or more hydrogen atoms are replaced by hydrocarbon groups or by the condensing or "stacking" of one or more rings. A simple example of this occurs in naphthalene (C_{10},H_8).

Naphthalene. As the molecular structure becomes characterized by denser carbon atoms and even further stacking, we enter the realm of "heavy oils". One of the most complex examples of "stacking" occurs in asphaltenes. Asphaltenes are distillation products from oil refineries that are used as asphalt on roads.

Thus, you can see that the number of hydrogen atoms associated with a given skeleton of carbon atoms may vary. When the chain or ring carries the full complement of hydrogen atoms, the hydrocarbon is said to be "saturated". When less than the full complement of hydrogen atoms is present in a hydrocarbon chain or ring, the hydrocarbon is said to be "unsaturated". These terms apply to both mineral oils and organic edible oils.

C.D. SHARBONO

All fossil fuels have played and still play important roles in providing the energy that every man, woman, and child in the United States uses every-day in today's world. With better technology for finding and using fossil fuels, each can play an equally important role in the future.

BIOGRAPHY - Carla Denise Sharbono, M.D.

Carla Denise is now a retired medical doctor who has renewed her interest in writing. She specializes in writing about subjects related to science, religion, medicine, nutrition, and safe and effective means of weight loss.

Born in Billings, Montana, Carla Denise graduated in 1965 from the Huntley Project High School in Worden, Montana. She then joined the U.S. Marine Corps and served from 1965 - 1968. After finishing her military obligation she used the GI Bill to obtain a college education. She received her BS degree in Health and Physical Education with a minor in Chemistry and Biology and began teaching science and health and physical education in 1971.

Carla Denise received her M.D. degree in 1986 from Louisiana State University Medical Center in Shreveport, La. In 1988, she received her Arkansas medical license and then moved to Arkansas where she began her medical practice in rural Arkansas.

Carla Denise is the proud and happy mother of 2 adult sons and a grandmother. Also, Carla is a member of Twin Lakes Marine and the Marine Corps League. As a veteran of the Vietnam era she continues to help veterans, especially with post traumatic issues and depression, overcome some of the issues that hinder them from achieving a better quality of life through diet, counseling and medication.

Her mission still remains "to serve others" by teaching or instructing them on how they can become a healthier individual by using natural (food) nutrients as well as teaching those who are interested in a Biblical explanation of the origins of life and the universe. As well as being interested in putting puzzles together with her family during wintery Montana days she was also interested in getting to the truth behind any idea or scientific theory or fact. She believes the Bible is the infallible word of God, and can be profitable for not only doctrine, but also for edification (intellectual, moral, or spiritual improvement) reproof, (correct gently) and instruction (knowledge or information to be imparted; usually, instructions, orders or directions with authority). She has studied the scriptures looking for a plausible answer as to "why the rocks and fossils found in them may be millions of years old and yet man as we know man who had the ability to write about history is only approximately 7,000 years old. This figure, 7000 years, goes along with the genealogy found in both the Old and New Testaments of the Bible. This book, her latest, "The World That Was - Before Adam and Eve" is the result of this search.